This Travel Log Belongs to

Begun: Completed:

Printed in the United States of America
First Printing, 2016

ISBN: 978-0-9890973-4-5
BISAC: TRV000000 Travel/General

Pyewacky Press
P.O. Box 265
Mendocino, CA 95460
katypye.com/pyewacky-press

Cover Illustration: © 2016 by Katy Pye
Cover design: Katy Pye; John C. Weston www.johncweston.com
Interior design & book production: Katy Pye and Pyewacky Press
Front Cover photographs: ©Katy Pye
Back Cover images: ©Katy Pye; lantern, lighthouse and map drawings: public domain
Author photo: Laurie MacMillan http://sunfielddesign.com/

Interior images attributions:

Point Cabrillo Light Station State Historic Park-lighthouse tower, lantern room, and 3rd order Fresnel lens: ©Katy Pye
Point Cabrillo Light Station State Historic Park-lighthouse lens: ©Katy Pye
Point Cabrillo Light Station State Historic Park-lighthouse and tall ship, *Lynx*: ©Katy Pye
Weather icon clipart: warszawianka, OpenClipart.org
Dogtooth violet: warszawianka, OpenClipart.org
Statue of Liberty Original torch light: Ad Meskens. Creative Commons Attribution-Share Alike 3.0 Unported https://commons.wikimedia.org/wiki/File:Original_torch_of_ Lady_Liberty_2.jpg. Edited to b&w
Sentinel Island Light: Gillphoto Creative Commons Attribution-Share Alike 3.0 https://upload. wikimedia.org/wikipedia/commons/2/22/Sentinel_Island_Light_Station_27.jpg. Edited to b&w, cropped
Point Cabrillo Light Station State Historic Park-lighthouse: ©Katy Pye
New London Ledge: Moondancedryad Creative Commons Attribution-Share Alike 3.0 https:// upload.wikimedia.org/wikipedia/commons/9/90/New_London_Ledge_Lighthouse.jpg. Edited to b&w, cropped
Tybee Island Light: Lawrence G. Miller Wikimedia Creative Commons: GNU Free https://up-load.wikimedia.org/wikipedia/commons/6/62/Tybeelight.jpg
Documentation License, Version 1.2 https://commons.wikimedia.org/wiki/File:Tybeelight.jpg. Edited to b&w
Grosse Point Lighthouse: Marit & Toomas Hinnosaar. Creative Commons Attribution 2.0 Generic. https://commons.wikimedia.org/wiki/File:Grosse_Point_Light_-_Evanston_IL. jpg. Edited to b&w

Dedicated to all the passionate "keepers."
Your love for lighthouses ensures their legacy
~the history, the stories, and the lights~shine on.

AN EYE ON HISTORY

Chance Brothers, 3rd order, Fresnel lens
Point Cabrillo Light Station State Historic Park, Mendocino, CA

Why Keep a Lighthouse Log?

Lighthouses are a visible and beloved part of our nation's history, yet they are steadily disappearing from use and public access. Luminous lenses are replaced by sterile beacons. Fog signals go silent. Lacking federal or private funds for upkeep or restoration, keeper's houses and entire lightstations are abandoned. Yet, there are beams, foghorns, and buildings that survive thanks to dedicated local and government groups, docents, volunteers, and visitor donations. The history and community surrounding these lucky lights beckon to you. Explore. Log and share their stories and your adventures.

How to use:

1) Plan a trip: by state, lens size, or lighthouse features, perhaps those known for their women lightkeepers, their age, or reported hauntings. Purely random, unplanned stops work well, too.

2) Record the lighthouse or station characteristics, history, surroundings, and other activities during your visit. Chronicle overnight or longer stays as a guest or volunteer keeper. Track treasures you purchase or light-house-themed collections, like stamps, ornaments or figurines.

3) Add your own creative spark: drawings, poems, photos.

There are thirty-two sections (four pages each) to document the lighthouses you visit. Each set also highlights one lighthouse by state, often with an historic U.S. Coast Guard image. The examples were chosen, in part, to illustrate different structural types, architectural designs, and time periods. Some locations are open to the public, some are not. Not all are the most famous, the most intact, or revered, but all are important measures of our past, present, and future. Don't feel confined to travel within the U.S. Use this log journal to capture your lighthouse visits anywhere in the world.

There are blank areas throughout to record experiences, thoughts, prose, poems or story ideas, artwork (pen or pencil work best), anything that moves you. Lighthouse books and Internet information sites abound. A few are included at the back along with a short glossary of terms.

Above all, have fun. Make this work your own or make it a family project. May it become a used and cherished keepsake.

Statue of Liberty
Original torch light

Boston almost claimed Liberty in 1882 when public funding in New York lagged. A New York Times editorial declared, "No third rate town is going to step in and take it from us." Authorized as a lighthouse by General Ulysses S. Grant so it could receive federal funding, he also chose Bedloe (now Liberty) Island, as its home. However, the light was never bright enough and Bedloe Island was too far inland to make it a useful beacon.

List of Lighthouses or Lightstations Visited

_____

_____

_____

_____

_____

_____

_____

_____

_____

_____

_____

_____

_____

_____

_____

_____

Pharologist

One who studies or is interested in lighthouses.

_____

_____

_____

_____

_____

_____

_____

_____

_____

_____

_____

_____

_____

_____

Middle Bay aka Mobile Bay Lighthouse
Mobile Bay, Alabama

Activated in 1885, this "screwpile" lighthouse used whale oil as its first fuel. Its signal was a 30 second red flash, plus a 5 second fog bell when needed. The auto beacon was deactivated in 1967. The lighthouse was added to the National Register of Historic Places in 1974. The original, 4th order Fresnel lens is on public loan to the Ft. Morgan Museum. The Alabama Historical Society began lighthouse restoration in 2009. Unfinished. Drive-by boat visits only. Charters available.

Weather ___ ☀ ___ ⛅ ___ 🌧 ___ 🌧 ___ 🌨

Lighthouse/Station _____

_____ Visit date _____

Location _____

Maintained by _____

☐ Restored/Date _____ ☐ Original lens still working

Fee/donation: $ _____ ☐ Docent/story teller

☐ Lighthouse ☐ Lightstation ☐ Originally a "family" or a
☐ "stag" lighthouse/station

Date built _____ Date originally lit _____

Illumination type (lens & order)_____

Signal characteristics _____

Focal plane _____Geographic range _____

Lens in operation from _____to _____

☐ Decommissioned/Date _____ ☐ Relit _____

☐ Lens removed from lantern room ☐ Displayed onsite or

☐ offsite _____

☐ Replaced by fixed beacon   ☐ No lens remains

Type of lamp(s) in its history _____

Fuels used in its history _____

Building materials _____

Height _____Overall condition _____

Historical total of Head lightkeepers _____
☐ Fog horns/signals ☐ Working
☐ Visited inside lighthouse ☐ Visited inside lantern room
☐ Walked on the lantern gallery ☐ Took photos
☐ Gift shop ☐ Purchase _____

_____

Favorite facts and lore _____

_____

_____

_____

_____

_____

_____

Special Events _____

_____

Nature, walks or other attractions during the visit

_____

_____

_____

Notes / Sketches / Photos / Postcard

In 1837, the Russians established Baranof Castle Lighthouse as an adminstration building near Sitka, Alaska. The U.S. gained control over the building when it bought Alaska in 1867. Sadly, a 1894 fire destroyed the castle lighthouse.

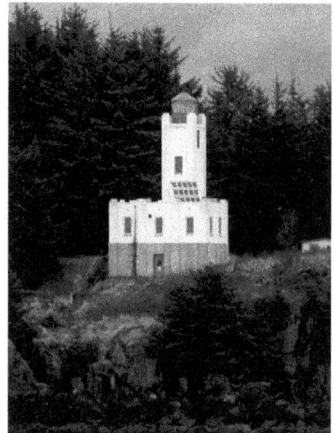

Sentinel Island, Juneau, Alaska 1902

1902. Inactive. Sentinel Island sits on an island at the northern end of Favorite Channel. The original 4th order Fresnel lens is on display at Alki Point Light in Seattle, Washington. This Art Deco style tower was added in 1935, and the lightkeepers house was burned down in 1971. Open to the public by appointment through the Gastineau Historical Society.

Weather ___ ☀ ___ ⛅ ___ 🌦 ___ 🌧 ___ 🌨

Lighthouse/Station _____

_____ Visit date _____

Location _____

Maintained by _____

☐ Restored/Date _____ ☐ Original lens still working

Fee/donation: $ _____ ☐ Docent/story teller

☐ Lighthouse ☐ Lightstation ☐ Originally a "family" or a
☐ "stag" lighthouse/station

Date built _____ Date originally lit _____

Illumination type (lens & order)_____

Signal characteristics _____

Focal plane _____Geographic range _____

Lens in operation from _____to _____

☐ Decommissioned/Date _____ ☐ Relit _____

☐ Lens removed from lantern room ☐ Displayed onsite or

☐ offsite _____

☐ Replaced by fixed beacon   ☐ No lens remains

Type of lamp(s) in its history _____

Fuels used in its history _____

Building materials _____

Height _____Overall condition _____

Historical total of Head lightkeepers _____
☐ Fog horns/signals   ☐ Working
☐ Visited inside lighthouse ☐ Visited inside lantern room
☐ Walked on the lantern gallery ☐ Took photos
☐ Gift shop ☐ Purchase _____

_____

Favorite facts and lore _____

_____

_____

_____

_____

_____

Special Events _____

_____

Nature, walks or other attractions during the visit

_____

_____

_____

More notes / Sketches / Photos / Postcards

Point Cabrillo Light Station State Historic Park - Mendocino, California

1909. Active. Decommissioned 1972. Light Station restored and relit in 1999. Original 3rd order, Chance Brothers, Fresnel lens. Active duty aid to navigation. State Park: 300 acres. Lighthouse interpretive center and gift shop, lightkeeper houses and buildings as museum and vacation rentals; saltwater tank and marine displays; nature trails. Whale watching. Open daily, lens tours several times a year. Managed by the Point Cabrillo Lightkeepers Association.

Weather ___ ☀ ___ ☁ ___ 🌧 ___ ⛈ ___ 🌨

Lighthouse/Station _____

_____ Visit date _____

Location _____

Maintained by _____

☐ Restored/Date _____ ☐ Original lens still working

Fee/donation: $ _____ ☐ Docent/story teller

☐ Lighthouse ☐ Lightstation ☐ Originally a "family" or a
☐ "stag" lighthouse/station

Date built _____ Date originally lit _____

Illumination type (lens & order)_____

Signal characteristics _____

Focal plane _____Geographic range _____

Lens in operation from _____to _____

☐ Decommissioned/Date _____ ☐ Relit _____

☐ Lens removed from lantern room ☐ Displayed onsite or

☐ offsite _____

☐ Replaced by fixed beacon ☐ No lens remains

Type of lamp(s) in its history _____

Fuels used in its history _____

Building materials _____

Height _____Overall condition _____

Historical total of Head lightkeepers _____
☐ Fog horns/signals   ☐ Working
☐ Visited inside lighthouse ☐ Visited inside lantern room
☐ Walked on the lantern gallery ☐ Took photos
☐ Gift shop ☐ Purchase _____

_____

Favorite facts and lore _____

_____

_____

_____

_____

_____

_____

Special Events _____

_____

Nature, walks or other attractions during the visit

_____

_____

_____

More notes / Sketches / Photos / Postcards

New London Ledge Light
New London, Connecticut

Established 1761. Empire-style building of 1909, now with solar-powered beacon. Restored by New London Ledge Lighthouse Foundation. 4th-order, Henry-Lepaute, Fresnel lens in the Custom House Museum of Maritime History. Interpretive center in lighthouse. "Project Oceanology" run for schools. Tours July-August by boat. Owned by the New London Maritime Society. Managed by the Foundation.

Weather ___ ☀ ___ ⛅ ___ 🌦 ___ 🌧 ___ 🌨

Lighthouse/Station _____

_____ Visit date _____

Location _____

Maintained by _____

☐ Restored/Date _____ ☐ Original lens still working

Fee/donation: $ _____ ☐ Docent/story teller

☐ Lighthouse ☐ Lightstation ☐ Originally a "family" or a
☐ "stag" lighthouse/station

Date built _____ Date originally lit _____

Illumination type (lens & order)_____

Signal characteristics _____

Focal plane _____Geographic range _____

Lens in operation from _____to _____

☐ Decommissioned/Date _____ ☐ Relit _____

☐ Lens removed from lantern room ☐ Displayed onsite or

☐ offsite _____

☐ Replaced by fixed beacon ☐ No lens remains

Type of lamp(s) in its history _____

Fuels used in its history _____

Building materials _____

Height _____Overall condition _____

Historical total of Head lightkeepers _____
☐ Fog horns/signals   ☐ Working
☐ Visited inside lighthouse ☐ Visited inside lantern room
☐ Walked on the lantern gallery   ☐ Took photos
☐ Gift shop ☐ Purchase _____

_____

Favorite facts and lore _____

_____

_____

_____

_____

_____

_____

Special Events _____

_____

Nature, walks or other attractions during the visit

_____

_____

_____

More notes / Sketches / Photos / Postcards

Fourteen Foot Bank Light
Delaware Bay, Delaware

1888; Active. "Caisson," aka "sparkplug" or "bug light". Solar powered beacon. 4th order Fresnel lens resides in the Cannonball House Maritime Museum in Lewes. Fog horn active. University of Delaware contracts space from private owner for environmental monitoring. Not open to the public.

Weather ___ ___ ___ ___ ___

Lighthouse/Station _____

_____ Visit date _____

Location _____

Maintained by _____

☐ Restored/Date _____ ☐ Original lens still working

Fee/donation: $ _____ ☐ Docent/story teller

☐ Lighthouse ☐ Lightstation ☐ Originally a "family" or a ☐ "stag" lighthouse/station

Date built _____ Date originally lit _____

Illumination type (lens & order)_____

Signal characteristics _____

Focal plane _____Geographic range _____

Lens in operation from _____to _____

☐ Decommissioned/Date _____ ☐ Relit _____

☐ Lens removed from lantern room ☐ Displayed onsite or

☐ offsite _____

☐ Replaced by fixed beacon ☐ No lens remains

Type of lamp(s) in its history _____

Fuels used in its history _____

Building materials _____

Height _____Overall condition _____

Historical total of Head lightkeepers _____
☐ Fog horns/signals   ☐ Working
☐ Visited inside lighthouse ☐ Visited inside lantern room
☐ Walked on the lantern gallery ☐ Took photos
☐ Gift shop ☐ Purchase _____

_____

Favorite facts and lore _____

_____

_____

_____

_____

_____

Special Events _____

_____

Nature, walks or other attractions during the visit

_____

_____

_____

More notes / Sketches / Photos / Postcards

Fuels used before lights were electrified: Whale oil, Colza oil (pressed wild cabbage), lard, and kerosene.

Jupiter Inlet Lighthouse - Jupiter, Florida

1860. Active. 1st order Fresnel lens in use. Museum in oil house. Renovated by state and USCG. In 2008 the lightstation and surrounding area were designated an Outstanding Natural Area. Federal funds restored lightstation and habitat. Open most days for tours. Bureau of Land Management and Loxahatchee River Historical Society co-manage.

Weather ___ ☀ ___ ⛅ ___ 🌦 ___ ⛈ ___ 🌨

Lighthouse/Station _____

_____ Visit date _____

Location _____

Maintained by _____

☐ Restored/Date _____ ☐ Original lens still working

Fee/donation: $ _____ ☐ Docent/story teller

☐ Lighthouse ☐ Lightstation ☐ Originally a "family" or a
☐ "stag" lighthouse/station

Date built _____ Date originally lit _____

Illumination type (lens & order)_____

Signal characteristics _____

Focal plane _____Geographic range _____

Lens in operation from _____to _____

☐ Decommissioned/Date _____ ☐ Relit _____

☐ Lens removed from lantern room ☐ Displayed onsite or

☐ offsite _____

☐ Replaced by fixed beacon ☐ No lens remains

Type of lamp(s) in its history _____

Fuels used in its history _____

Building materials _____

Height _____Overall condition _____

Historical total of Head lightkeepers _____
☐ Fog horns/signals   ☐ Working
☐ Visited inside lighthouse ☐ Visited inside lantern room
☐ Walked on the lantern gallery ☐ Took photos
☐ Gift shop ☐ Purchase _____

_____

Favorite facts and lore _____

_____

_____

_____

_____

_____

_____

Special Events _____

_____

Nature, walks or other attractions during the visit

_____

_____

_____

More notes / Sketches / Photos / Postcards

Fresnel lenses illuminate with different beam patterns: "flashing light," "fixed light," and "occulting light." Sometimes color is added to the light's characteristic flash pattern.

Tybee Island Range Rear Light
Tybee, Georgia

Established 1732. Active, its 1st order Fresnel lens (1867) is still in use. Second-oldest lighthouse in the nation. Current octagonal light rebuilt in 1867. It was partially burned during the Civil War to keep the Union Army from signaling its ships. Open most days. Self-guided tour to the top. Managed by the Tybee Island Historical Society.

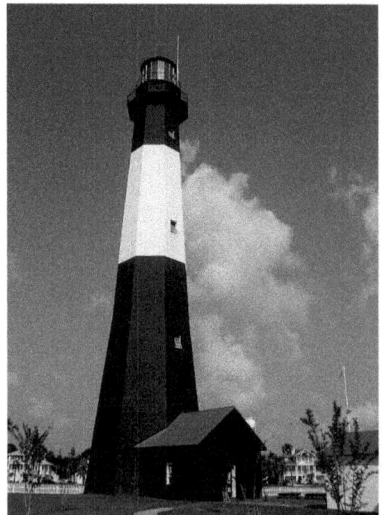

Weather ___ ☀ ___ ⛅ ___ ⛈ ___ 🌧 ___ 🌨

Lighthouse/Station _____

_____ Visit date _____

Location _____

Maintained by _____

☐ Restored/Date _____ ☐ Original lens still working

Fee/donation: $ _____ ☐ Docent/story teller

☐ Lighthouse ☐ Lightstation ☐ Originally a "family" or a
☐ "stag" lighthouse/station

Date built _____ Date originally lit _____

Illumination type (lens & order)_____

Signal characteristics _____

Focal plane _____Geographic range _____

Lens in operation from _____to _____

☐ Decommissioned/Date _____ ☐ Relit _____

☐ Lens removed from lantern room ☐ Displayed onsite or

☐ offsite _____

☐ Replaced by fixed beacon   ☐ No lens remains

Type of lamp(s) in its history _____

Fuels used in its history _____

Building materials _____

Height _____Overall condition _____

Historical total of Head lightkeepers _____
☐ Fog horns/signals   ☐ Working
☐ Visited inside lighthouse ☐ Visited inside lantern room
☐ Walked on the lantern gallery ☐ Took photos
☐ Gift shop ☐ Purchase _____

_____

Favorite facts and lore _____

_____

_____

_____

_____

_____

_____

Special Events _____

_____

Nature, walks or other attractions during the visit

_____

_____

_____

More notes / Sketches / Photos / Postcards

Kīlauea Point Lighthouse
Kauai'i, Hawai'i

1913. Active after being closed 1976-2013.
Reinforced concrete tower. In situ 2nd
order Fresnel lens. Original keeper's and
accessory buildings. Kīlauea Point Natural
History Association completed restoration
in 2013. National Register of Historic
Places. Reactivated and dedicated as
the Daniel K. Inoye Kīlauea Point Lighthouse. Site of Kīlauea Point National
Wildlife Refuge. Open weekdays. Tower
tour once-a-year in May.

Weather ___ ☀ ___ ⛅ ___ 🌧 ___ ⛈ ___ 🌨

Lighthouse/Station _____

_____ Visit date _____

Location _____

Maintained by _____

☐ Restored/Date _____ ☐ Original lens still working

Fee/donation: $ _____ ☐ Docent/story teller

☐ Lighthouse ☐ Lightstation ☐ Originally a "family" or a
☐ "stag" lighthouse/station

Date built _____ Date originally lit _____

Illumination type (lens & order)_____

Signal characteristics _____

Focal plane _____Geographic range _____

Lens in operation from _____to _____

☐ Decommissioned/Date _____ ☐ Relit _____

☐ Lens removed from lantern room ☐ Displayed onsite or

☐ offsite _____

☐ Replaced by fixed beacon   ☐ No lens remains

Type of lamp(s) in its history _____

Fuels used in its history _____

Building materials _____

Height _____Overall condition _____

Historical total of Head lightkeepers _____
☐ Fog horns/signals   ☐ Working
☐ Visited inside lighthouse ☐ Visited inside lantern room
☐ Walked on the lantern gallery ☐ Took photos
☐ Gift shop ☐ Purchase _____

_____

Favorite facts and lore _____

_____

_____

_____

_____

_____

Special Events _____

_____

Nature, walks or other attractions during the visit

_____

_____

_____

More notes / Sketches / Photos / Postcards

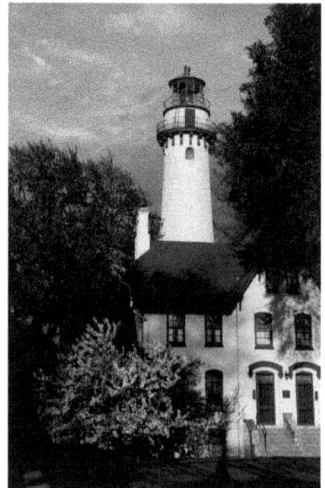

Grosse Point Light
Evanston, Illinois

1873. Reactivated after WWII. Original 1850,
2nd order, Henry-Lepaute Fresnel lens in use.
Two fog signal buildings. National Historic Landmark, museum, visitor, and nature centers. Lighthouse renovated 2013. Guided seasonal tower
tours. Lens privately maintained. Owner: City of
Evanston. Manager: Lighthouse Park District.

Weather ___ ☀ ___ ⛅ ___ 🌧 ___ ⛈ ___ 🌨

Lighthouse/Station _____

_____ Visit date _____

Location _____

Maintained by _____

☐ Restored/Date _____ ☐ Original lens still working

Fee/donation: $ _____ ☐ Docent/story teller

☐ Lighthouse ☐ Lightstation ☐ Originally a "family" or a
☐ "stag" lighthouse/station

Date built _____ Date originally lit _____

Illumination type (lens & order)_____

Signal characteristics _____

Focal plane _____Geographic range _____

Lens in operation from _____to _____

☐ Decommissioned/Date _____ ☐ Relit _____

☐ Lens removed from lantern room ☐ Displayed onsite or

☐ offsite _____

☐ Replaced by fixed beacon ☐ No lens remains

Type of lamp(s) in its history _____

Fuels used in its history _____

Building materials _____

Height _____Overall condition _____

Historical total of Head lightkeepers _____
☐ Fog horns/signals   ☐ Working
☐ Visited inside lighthouse ☐ Visited inside lantern room
☐ Walked on the lantern gallery ☐ Took photos
☐ Gift shop ☐ Purchase _____

_____

Favorite facts and lore _____

_____

_____

_____

_____

_____

_____

Special Events _____

_____

Nature, walks or other attractions during the visit

_____

_____

_____

More notes / Sketches / Photos / Postcards

The Old Michigan City Light has known two women lightkeepers: Mrs. Harriet C. Towner -1844 to 1853 and Harriet E. Colfax 1861 to 1904.

Old Michigan City Light
Michigan City, Indiana

Station established 1835. Inactive since 1904, this brick and wood keeper's house dates from 1858 and remained in use until 1940. Cylindrical wooden tower attached. Michigan City Old Lighthouse Museum has the 5th order L. Sautter Fresnel lens on display. Museum and tower open to public afternoons except Monday. Managed by the Michigan City Historical Society.

Weather ___ ☀ ___ ⛅ ___ ⛈ ___ 🌧 ___ 🌨

Lighthouse/Station _____

_____ Visit date _____

Location _____

Maintained by _____

☐ Restored/Date _____ ☐ Original lens still working

Fee/donation: $ _____ ☐ Docent/story teller

☐ Lighthouse ☐ Lightstation ☐ Originally a "family" or a
☐ "stag" lighthouse/station

Date built _____ Date originally lit _____

Illumination type (lens & order) _____

Signal characteristics _____

Focal plane _____ Geographic range _____

Lens in operation from _____ to _____

☐ Decommissioned/Date _____ ☐ Relit _____

☐ Lens removed from lantern room ☐ Displayed onsite or

☐ offsite _____

☐ Replaced by fixed beacon ☐ No lens remains

Type of lamp(s) in its history _____

Fuels used in its history _____

Building materials _____

Height _____ Overall condition _____

Historical total of Head lightkeepers _____

☐ Fog horns/signals ☐ Working

☐ Visited inside lighthouse ☐ Visited inside lantern room

☐ Walked on the lantern gallery ☐ Took photos

☐ Gift shop ☐ Purchase _____

_____

Favorite facts and lore _____

_____

_____

_____

_____

_____

_____

Special Events _____

_____

Nature, walks or other attractions during the visit

_____

_____

_____

More notes / Sketches / Photos / Postcards

New Canal, Lake Ponchetrain
New Orleans, Louisiana

Established 1838, rebuilt 1890. After great
effort, the lighthouse was reconstructed,
rededicated and relit in 2012 post
hurricanes Rita and Katrina. The Lake
Pontchartrain Basin Foundation restored
and maintains The New Canal Lighthouse
Museum and Education Center. Historical
and ecological displays. Open daily
except Sunday.

Weather ___ ☀ ___ ⛅ ___ 🌦 ___ 🌧 ___ 🌨

Lighthouse/Station _____

_____ Visit date _____

Location _____

Maintained by _____

☐ Restored/Date _____   ☐ Original lens still working

Fee/donation: $ _____   ☐ Docent/story teller

☐ Lighthouse ☐ Lightstation ☐ Originally a "family" or a
☐ "stag" lighthouse/station

Date built _____ Date originally lit _____

Illumination type (lens & order)_____

Signal characteristics _____

Focal plane _____Geographic range _____

Lens in operation from _____to _____

☐ Decommissioned/Date _____ ☐ Relit _____

☐ Lens removed from lantern room ☐ Displayed onsite or

☐ offsite _____

☐ Replaced by fixed beacon   ☐ No lens remains

Type of lamp(s) in its history _____

Fuels used in its history _____

Building materials _____

Height _____Overall condition _____

Historical total of Head lightkeepers _____
☐ Fog horns/signals   ☐ Working
☐ Visited inside lighthouse ☐ Visited inside lantern room
☐ Walked on the lantern gallery ☐ Took photos
☐ Gift shop ☐ Purchase _____

_____

Favorite facts and lore _____

_____

_____

_____

_____

_____

_____

Special Events _____

_____

Nature, walks or other attractions during the visit

_____

_____

_____

More notes / Sketches / Photos / Postcards

Rockland Breakwater Light
Rockland, Maine

Completed and lit 1902. Breakwater,
seven-eighths of a mile long by twenty feet
wide. Fourth order Fresnel lens and first-
class Daboll trumpet fog signal and later a
fog bell. Automated 1965. Maintained by
the Friends of Rockland Harbor Lights.
Maine Lighthouse Museum in Rockland
has lighthouse artifacts.

Weather ___ ☀ ___ ⛅ ___ 🌧 ___ ⛈ ___ 🌨

Lighthouse/Station _____

_____ Visit date _____

Location _____

Maintained by _____

☐ Restored/Date _____ ☐ Original lens still working

Fee/donation: $ _____ ☐ Docent/story teller

☐ Lighthouse ☐ Lightstation ☐ Originally a "family" or a
☐ "stag" lighthouse/station

Date built _____ Date originally lit _____

Illumination type (lens & order)_____

Signal characteristics _____

Focal plane _____Geographic range _____

Lens in operation from _____to _____

☐ Decommissioned/Date _____ ☐ Relit _____

☐ Lens removed from lantern room ☐ Displayed onsite or

☐ offsite _____

☐ Replaced by fixed beacon ☐ No lens remains

Type of lamp(s) in its history _____

Fuels used in its history _____

Building materials _____

Height _____Overall condition _____

Historical total of Head lightkeepers _____
☐ Fog horns/signals   ☐ Working
☐ Visited inside lighthouse ☐ Visited inside lantern room
☐ Walked on the lantern gallery ☐ Took photos
☐ Gift shop ☐ Purchase _____

_____

Favorite facts and lore _____

_____

_____

_____

_____

_____

_____

Special Events _____

_____

Nature, walks or other attractions during the visit

_____

_____

_____

More notes / Sketches / Photos / Postcards

Hooper Strait Lighthouse
Chesapeake Bay, Maryland

Lit 1879, staffed until 1954. "Cottage-style,"
screwpile light. Saved in1966 from dem-
olition. The lighthouse was raised off its
deteriorating pilings and barged to Navy
Point where it was re-erected over dry land.
Now the Chesapeake Bay Marine Museum,
it houses a unique Fresnel lens whose
flashing pattern was CBMM in Morse code.

Weather ___ ☀ ___ ⛅ ___ 🌧 ___ 🌧 ___ 🌧

Lighthouse/Station _____

_____ Visit date _____

Location _____

Maintained by _____

☐ Restored/Date _____ ☐ Original lens still working

Fee/donation: $ _____ ☐ Docent/story teller

☐ Lighthouse ☐ Lightstation ☐ Originally a "family" or a
☐ "stag" lighthouse/station

Date built _____ Date originally lit _____

Illumination type (lens & order)_____

Signal characteristics _____

Focal plane _____Geographic range _____

Lens in operation from _____to _____

☐ Decommissioned/Date _____ ☐ Relit _____

☐ Lens removed from lantern room ☐ Displayed onsite or

☐ offsite _____

☐ Replaced by fixed beacon ☐ No lens remains

Type of lamp(s) in its history _____

Fuels used in its history _____

Building materials _____

Height _____Overall condition _____

Historical total of Head lightkeepers _____

☐ Fog horns/signals   ☐ Working

☐ Visited inside lighthouse ☐ Visited inside lantern room

☐ Walked on the lantern gallery ☐ Took photos

☐ Gift shop ☐ Purchase _____

_____

Favorite facts and lore _____

_____

_____

_____

_____

_____

_____

Special Events _____

_____

Nature, walks or other attractions during the visit

_____

_____

_____

More notes / Sketches / Photos / Postcards

The only remaining manned lighthouse is Boston Light on Little Brewster Island. The original, the first built on U.S. soil in 1716, was destroyed during the Revolution (1776).

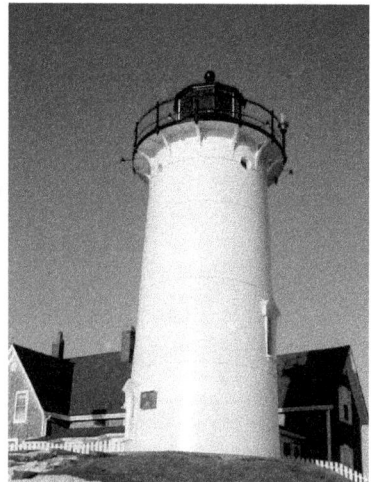

Nobska Point Light
Woods Hole, Massachusetts

Established 1829, current light lit in 1876. Active. An 1888, 4th order, Fresnel lens and fog horn in use. National Register of Historic Places. A 2015 license agreement gives the U.S. Coast Guard, the Town of Falmouth, and Friends of Nobska Light a working restoration and management future. Site open daily. Light occasionally. Manager U.S. Coast Guard.

Weather ___ ☀ ___ ⛅ ___ 🌦 ___ 🌧 ___ 🌨

Lighthouse/Station _____

_____ Visit date _____

Location _____

Maintained by _____

☐ Restored/Date _____ ☐ Original lens still working

Fee/donation: $ _____ ☐ Docent/story teller

☐ Lighthouse ☐ Lightstation ☐ Originally a "family" or a
☐ "stag" lighthouse/station

Date built _____ Date originally lit _____

Illumination type (lens & order)_____

Signal characteristics _____

Focal plane _____Geographic range _____

Lens in operation from _____to _____

☐ Decommissioned/Date _____ ☐ Relit _____

☐ Lens removed from lantern room ☐ Displayed onsite or

☐ offsite _____

☐ Replaced by fixed beacon ☐ No lens remains

Type of lamp(s) in its history _____

Fuels used in its history _____

Building materials _____

Height _____Overall condition _____

Historical total of Head lightkeepers _____
☐ Fog horns/signals   ☐ Working
☐ Visited inside lighthouse   ☐ Visited inside lantern room
☐ Walked on the lantern gallery   ☐ Took photos
☐ Gift shop ☐ Purchase _____

_____

Favorite facts and lore _____

_____

_____

_____

_____

_____

_____

Special Events _____

_____

Nature, walks or other attractions during the visit

_____

_____

_____

More notes / Sketches / Photos / Postcards

Tawas Point Light
Iosco County, Michigan

1876. Active. Original 4th order lens in use,
but in October 2015, the U.S. Coast Guard
announced a decommission plan for the lighthouse, including removal and replacement of
the lens with a modern beacon. Site and tower
open daily in season. Volunteer keepers can
stay up to 2 weeks. Managed by Tawas Point
State Park.

Weather ___ ☀ ___ ⛅ ___ 🌧 ___ 🌧 ___ 🌨

Lighthouse/Station _____

_____ Visit date _____

Location _____

Maintained by _____

☐ Restored/Date _____ ☐ Original lens still working

Fee/donation: $ _____ ☐ Docent/story teller

☐ Lighthouse ☐ Lightstation ☐ Originally a "family" or a
☐ "stag" lighthouse/station

Date built _____ Date originally lit _____

Illumination type (lens & order)_____

Signal characteristics _____

Focal plane _____Geographic range _____

Lens in operation from _____to _____

☐ Decommissioned/Date _____ ☐ Relit _____

☐ Lens removed from lantern room ☐ Displayed onsite or

☐ offsite _____

☐ Replaced by fixed beacon   ☐ No lens remains

Type of lamp(s) in its history _____

Fuels used in its history _____

Building materials _____

Height _____Overall condition _____

Historical total of Head lightkeepers _____
☐ Fog horns/signals   ☐ Working
☐ Visited inside lighthouse ☐ Visited inside lantern room
☐ Walked on the lantern gallery ☐ Took photos
☐ Gift shop ☐ Purchase _____

_____

Favorite facts and lore _____

_____

_____

_____

_____

_____

_____

Special Events _____

_____

Nature, walks or other attractions during the visit

_____

_____

_____

More notes / Sketches / Photos / Postcards

The Great Lakes shores host the most lighthouses in the nation. By the beginning of the 20th century, there were 334 major lights and 67 fog signals.

Split Rock Light
Lake County, Minnesota

1910. Overlooking Lake Superior. Inactive since 1969, but the 3rd order, Barbier Benard & Turenne, bivalve, Fresnel lens is lit on special occasions. One is November 10th in memory of the ore carrier, *Edmund Fitzgerald*. Keepers' houses are a maritime museum. Owner: Minnesota Department of Natural Resources. Minnesota Historical Society site manager. Open daily in season.

Weather ___ ☀ ___ ⛅ ___ 🌧 ___ 🌧 ___ 🌨

Lighthouse/Station _____

_____ Visit date _____

Location _____

Maintained by _____

☐ Restored/Date _____ ☐ Original lens still working

Fee/donation: $ _____ ☐ Docent/story teller

☐ Lighthouse ☐ Lightstation ☐ Originally a "family" or a
☐ "stag" lighthouse/station

Date built _____ Date originally lit _____

Illumination type (lens & order)_____

Signal characteristics _____

Focal plane _____Geographic range _____

Lens in operation from _____to _____

☐ Decommissioned/Date _____ ☐ Relit _____

☐ Lens removed from lantern room ☐ Displayed onsite or

☐ offsite _____

☐ Replaced by fixed beacon ☐ No lens remains

Type of lamp(s) in its history _____

Fuels used in its history _____

Building materials _____

Height _____Overall condition _____

Historical total of Head lightkeepers _____

☐ Fog horns/signals   ☐ Working

☐ Visited inside lighthouse   ☐ Visited inside lantern room

☐ Walked on the lantern gallery   ☐ Took photos

☐ Gift shop ☐ Purchase _____

_____

Favorite facts and lore _____

_____

_____

_____

_____

_____

_____

Special Events _____

_____

Nature, walks or other attractions during the visit

_____

_____

_____

More notes / Sketches / Photos / Postcards

Biloxi Light - Biloxi, Mississippi

1848. Active, using a 1926 5th order Fresnel lens. The country's second-oldest cast iron lighthouse. Hurricane Camille (1969) destroyed the keepers' houses. Hurricane Katrina destroyed most of Biloxi and damaged the tower. After repairs, the light was relit in 2010. Site open daily. Tower open early mornings.

Weather ___ ☀ ___ ⛅ ___ 🌧 ___ 🌧 ___ 🌨

Lighthouse/Station _____

_____ Visit date _____

Location _____

Maintained by _____

☐ Restored/Date _____ ☐ Original lens still working

Fee/donation: $ _____ ☐ Docent/story teller

☐ Lighthouse ☐ Lightstation ☐ Originally a "family" or a ☐ "stag" lighthouse/station

Date built _____ Date originally lit _____

Illumination type (lens & order)_____

Signal characteristics _____

Focal plane _____ Geographic range _____

Lens in operation from _____ to _____

☐ Decommissioned/Date _____ ☐ Relit _____

☐ Lens removed from lantern room ☐ Displayed onsite or

☐ offsite _____

☐ Replaced by fixed beacon ☐ No lens remains

Type of lamp(s) in its history _____

Fuels used in its history _____

Building materials _____

Height _____ Overall condition _____

Historical total of Head lightkeepers _____
☐ Fog horns/signals   ☐ Working
☐ Visited inside lighthouse   ☐ Visited inside lantern room
☐ Walked on the lantern gallery   ☐ Took photos
☐ Gift shop ☐ Purchase _____

_____

Favorite facts and lore _____

_____

_____

_____

_____

_____

_____

Special Events _____

_____

Nature, walks or other attractions during the visit

_____

_____

_____

More notes / Sketches / Photos / Postcards

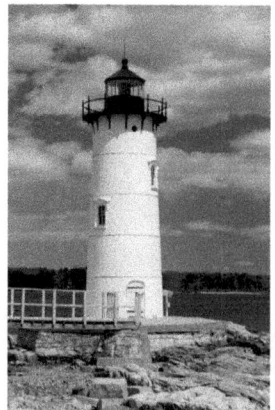

Portsmouth Harbor Lighthouse
New Castle, New Hampshire

Station established 1771. Several replacement towers,
current built in 1878. Active. 4th-order, Fresnel lens
(post 1935) converted into a fixed green light. Fog
horn. Exhibits in restored oil house. Keeper's house
used as offices by the U.S.C.G. offices. Located in Fort
Constitution State Historic Site. National Register
of Historic Places. Maintained by Friends of Portsmouth Harbor Lighthouses. Occasional tours.

Weather ___ ☀ ___ ⛅ ___ 🌧 ___ ⛈ ___ 🌨

Lighthouse/Station _____

_____ Visit date _____

Location _____

Maintained by _____

☐ Restored/Date _____ ☐ Original lens still working

Fee/donation: $ _____ ☐ Docent/story teller

☐ Lighthouse ☐ Lightstation ☐ Originally a "family" or a
☐ "stag" lighthouse/station

Date built _____ Date originally lit _____

Illumination type (lens & order)_____

Signal characteristics _____

Focal plane _____Geographic range _____

Lens in operation from _____to _____

☐ Decommissioned/Date _____ ☐ Relit _____

☐ Lens removed from lantern room ☐ Displayed onsite or

☐ offsite _____

☐ Replaced by fixed beacon   ☐ No lens remains

Type of lamp(s) in its history _____

Fuels used in its history _____

Building materials _____

Height _____Overall condition _____

Historical total of Head lightkeepers _____
☐ Fog horns/signals   ☐ Working
☐ Visited inside lighthouse ☐ Visited inside lantern room
☐ Walked on the lantern gallery ☐ Took photos
☐ Gift shop ☐ Purchase _____

_____

Favorite facts and lore _____

_____

_____

_____

_____

_____

_____

Special Events _____

_____

Nature, walks or other attractions during the visit

_____

_____

_____

More notes / Sketches / Photos / Postcards

Navesink Twin Towers, Higlands N.J., was the first U.S. lightstation fitted with a Fresnel lens (1841). 1st order, clamshell style now housed in an onsite display. The station was also the first to use kerosene (1883) and to install electric power (1898).

Sandy Hook Light
Highlands, New Jersey

1764. Sandy Hook is the oldest active lighthouse in the U.S. The only standing colonial period tower. 3rd order Fresnel lens (1857). National Historic Landmark. Part of the Gateway National Recreation Area (manager). Octagonal, brick-lined with rubblestone exterior. Victorian keeper's house (1883) is the visitor's center. Open daily.

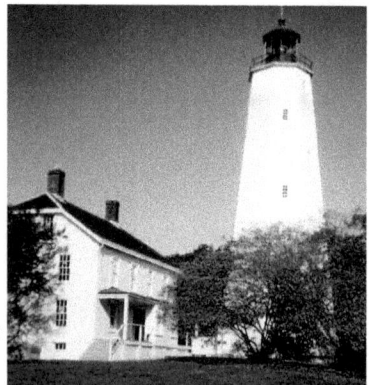

Weather ___ ☀ ___ ⛅ ___ 🌧 ___ 🌧 ___ 🌨

Lighthouse/Station _____

_____ Visit date _____

Location _____

Maintained by _____

☐ Restored/Date _____ ☐ Original lens still working

Fee/donation: $ _____ ☐ Docent/story teller

☐ Lighthouse ☐ Lightstation ☐ Originally a "family" or a
☐ "stag" lighthouse/station

Date built _____ Date originally lit _____

Illumination type (lens & order)_____

Signal characteristics _____

Focal plane _____Geographic range _____

Lens in operation from _____to _____

☐ Decommissioned/Date _____ ☐ Relit _____

☐ Lens removed from lantern room ☐ Displayed onsite or

☐ offsite _____

☐ Replaced by fixed beacon   ☐ No lens remains

Type of lamp(s) in its history _____

Fuels used in its history _____

Building materials _____

Height _____Overall condition _____

Historical total of Head lightkeepers _____
☐ Fog horns/signals   ☐ Working
☐ Visited inside lighthouse ☐ Visited inside lantern room
☐ Walked on the lantern gallery   ☐ Took photos
☐ Gift shop ☐ Purchase _____

_____

Favorite facts and lore _____

_____

_____

_____

_____

_____

_____

Special Events _____

_____

Nature, walks or other attractions during the visit

_____

_____

_____

More notes / Sketches / Photos / Postcards

Dunkirk Point aka Point Gratiot Light
Dunkirk, New York

Station established 1827. Active. Original 3rd
order Fresnel lens. Current buildings
and square, brick-clad rubblestone tower
constructed 1857. In 2010, the foundation of
the 1827 tower believed found. An archealog-
ical project was begun to verify. Museum and
tower open daily in season.

Weather __ ☀ __ ⛅ __ 🌧 __ 🌧 __ 🌨

Lighthouse/Station _____

_____ Visit date _____

Location _____

Maintained by _____

☐ Restored/Date _____   ☐ Original lens still working

Fee/donation: $ _____   ☐ Docent/story teller

☐ Lighthouse ☐ Lightstation ☐ Originally a "family" or a
☐ "stag" lighthouse/station

Date built _____ Date originally lit _____

Illumination type (lens & order)_____

Signal characteristics _____

Focal plane _____Geographic range _____

Lens in operation from _____to _____

☐ Decommissioned/Date _____ ☐ Relit _____

☐ Lens removed from lantern room ☐ Displayed onsite or

☐ offsite _____

☐ Replaced by fixed beacon   ☐ No lens remains

Type of lamp(s) in its history _____

Fuels used in its history _____

Building materials _____

Height _____Overall condition _____

Historical total of Head lightkeepers _____
☐ Fog horns/signals   ☐ Working
☐ Visited inside lighthouse ☐ Visited inside lantern room
☐ Walked on the lantern gallery ☐ Took photos
☐ Gift shop ☐ Purchase _____

_____

Favorite facts and lore _____

_____

_____

_____

_____

_____

Special Events _____

_____

Nature, walks or other attractions during the visit

_____

_____

_____

More notes / Sketches / Photos / Postcards

Currituck Beach Lighthouse
Corolla, North Carolina

1875. Active. Original 1st order Fresnel lens in use. Unpainted brick. Principal lightkeeper's, assistant's, and oil houses. Outer Banks Conservationists (OBC), Inc. restored the lightstation, which earned a spot on the National Register of Historic Places. Lightstation and tower open spring through fall.

Weather ___ ☀ ___ ☁ ___ 🌧 ___ ⛈ ___ 🌨

Lighthouse/Station _____

_____ Visit date _____

Location _____

Maintained by _____

☐ Restored/Date _____ ☐ Original lens still working

Fee/donation: $ _____ ☐ Docent/story teller

☐ Lighthouse ☐ Lightstation ☐ Originally a "family" or a
☐ "stag" lighthouse/station

Date built _____ Date originally lit _____

Illumination type (lens & order)_____

Signal characteristics _____

Focal plane _____Geographic range _____

Lens in operation from _____to _____

☐ Decommissioned/Date _____ ☐ Relit _____

☐ Lens removed from lantern room ☐ Displayed onsite or

☐ offsite _____

☐ Replaced by fixed beacon   ☐ No lens remains

Type of lamp(s) in its history _____

Fuels used in its history _____

Building materials _____

Height _____Overall condition _____

Historical total of Head lightkeepers _____
☐ Fog horns/signals   ☐ Working
☐ Visited inside lighthouse ☐ Visited inside lantern room
☐ Walked on the lantern gallery   ☐ Took photos
☐ Gift shop ☐ Purchase _____

_____

Favorite facts and lore _____

_____

_____

_____

_____

_____

_____

Special Events _____

_____

Nature, walks or other attractions during the visit

_____

_____

_____

More notes / Sketches / Photos / Postcards

Marblehead Lighthouse
Sandusky Bay, Ohio

1821. Active. Round, limestone tower.
The oldest active lighthouse on the U.S.
side of the Great Lakes. Third-order Fresnel
lens and mechanism on display. Victorian
replacement keeper's house museum and
tower open in season. Maintained by the
Marblehead Lighthouse Historical Society.

Weather ___ ☀ ___ ⛅ ___ 🌧 ___ 🌧 ___ 🌨

Lighthouse/Station _____

_____ Visit date _____

Location _____

Maintained by _____

☐ Restored/Date _____ ☐ Original lens still working

Fee/donation: $ _____ ☐ Docent/story teller

☐ Lighthouse ☐ Lightstation ☐ Originally a "family" or a
☐ "stag" lighthouse/station

Date built _____ Date originally lit _____

Illumination type (lens & order)_____

Signal characteristics _____

Focal plane _____Geographic range _____

Lens in operation from _____to _____

☐ Decommissioned/Date _____ ☐ Relit _____

☐ Lens removed from lantern room ☐ Displayed onsite or

☐ offsite _____

☐ Replaced by fixed beacon ☐ No lens remains

Type of lamp(s) in its history _____

Fuels used in its history _____

Building materials _____

Height _____Overall condition _____

Historical total of Head lightkeepers _____
☐ Fog horns/signals   ☐ Working
☐ Visited inside lighthouse ☐ Visited inside lantern room
☐ Walked on the lantern gallery ☐ Took photos
☐ Gift shop ☐ Purchase _____

_____

Favorite facts and lore _____

_____

_____

_____

_____

_____

_____

Special Events _____

_____

Nature, walks or other attractions during the visit

_____

_____

_____

More notes / Sketches / Photos / Postcards

Yaquina Head Freeport, Oregon

1873. Active. 1868 Barbier & Fenestre 1st order
Fresnel lens in use. Assistant lightkeeper's house
and several outbuildings remain. The site and
Yaquina Head Outstanding Natural Area are open
daily. Lighthouse tours limited days and hours.
Maintained by Friends of Yaquina Lighthouses.

Weather ___ ☀ ___ ⛅ ___ 🌧 ___ ⛈ ___ 🌨

Lighthouse/Station _____

_____ Visit date _____

Location _____

Maintained by _____

☐ Restored/Date _____ ☐ Original lens still working

Fee/donation: $ _____ ☐ Docent/story teller

☐ Lighthouse ☐ Lightstation ☐ Originally a "family" or a
☐ "stag" lighthouse/station

Date built _____ Date originally lit _____

Illumination type (lens & order)_____

Signal characteristics _____

Focal plane _____Geographic range _____

Lens in operation from _____to _____

☐ Decommissioned/Date _____ ☐ Relit _____

☐ Lens removed from lantern room ☐ Displayed onsite or

☐ offsite _____

☐ Replaced by fixed beacon   ☐ No lens remains

Type of lamp(s) in its history _____

Fuels used in its history _____

Building materials _____

Height _____Overall condition _____

Historical total of Head lightkeepers _____
☐ Fog horns/signals   ☐ Working
☐ Visited inside lighthouse ☐ Visited inside lantern room
☐ Walked on the lantern gallery ☐ Took photos
☐ Gift shop ☐ Purchase _____

_____

Favorite facts and lore _____

_____

_____

_____

_____

_____

Special Events _____

_____

Nature, walks or other attractions during the visit

_____

_____

_____

More notes / Sketches / Photos / Postcards

Range of building materials used in lighthouse construction: wood, brick, cut stone, cast and wrought iron, iron-clad brick, steel, reinforced concrete, aluminumn, and fiberglass.

Presque Isle Light Station
Lake Erie, Pennsylvania

1873, Active. Presque Isle State Park.
Tower-square cylindrical brick. Height raised
33 ft. in 1896. Restoration to reflect the 1900s
is planned by the Keepers of the Erie Lights.
The non-profit Presque Isle Light Station
leases the lighthouse and offers limited tours.

Weather ___ ☀ ___ ⛅ ___ 🌧 ___ 🌧 ___ 🌨

Lighthouse/Station _____

_____ Visit date _____

Location _____

Maintained by _____

☐ Restored/Date _____ ☐ Original lens still working

Fee/donation: $ _____ ☐ Docent/story teller

☐ Lighthouse ☐ Lightstation ☐ Originally a "family" or a
☐ "stag" lighthouse/station

Date built _____ Date originally lit _____

Illumination type (lens & order)_____

Signal characteristics _____

Focal plane _____Geographic range _____

Lens in operation from _____to _____

☐ Decommissioned/Date _____ ☐ Relit _____

☐ Lens removed from lantern room ☐ Displayed onsite or

☐ offsite _____

☐ Replaced by fixed beacon ☐ No lens remains

Type of lamp(s) in its history _____

Fuels used in its history _____

Building materials _____

Height _____Overall condition _____

Historical total of Head lightkeepers _____
☐ Fog horns/signals   ☐ Working
☐ Visited inside lighthouse ☐ Visited inside lantern room
☐ Walked on the lantern gallery   ☐ Took photos
☐ Gift shop ☐ Purchase _____

_____

Favorite facts and lore _____

_____

_____

_____

_____

_____

_____

Special Events _____

_____

Nature, walks or other attractions during the visit

_____

_____

_____

More notes / Sketches / Photos / Postcards

Block Island North - Block Island National
Wildlife Refuge
New Shoreham, Rhode Island

1868. Reactivated. Octagonal, cylindrical brick tower.
One-story, granite, "schoolhouse style" building attached to two-story keeper's house. This is the fourth,
successive lighthouse built at Block Island. Original
4th order Fresnel lens on display. Restored. Site and
museum open seasonally. Tower closed.

Weather ___ ☀ ___ ⛅ ___ 🌦 ___ 🌧 ___ 🌨

Lighthouse/Station _____

_____ Visit date _____

Location _____

Maintained by _____

☐ Restored/Date _____ ☐ Original lens still working

Fee/donation: $ _____ ☐ Docent/story teller

☐ Lighthouse ☐ Lightstation ☐ Originally a "family" or a
☐ "stag" lighthouse/station

Date built _____ Date originally lit _____

Illumination type (lens & order)_____

Signal characteristics _____

Focal plane _____Geographic range _____

Lens in operation from _____to _____

☐ Decommissioned/Date _____ ☐ Relit _____

☐ Lens removed from lantern room ☐ Displayed onsite or

☐ offsite _____

☐ Replaced by fixed beacon ☐ No lens remains

Type of lamp(s) in its history _____

Fuels used in its history _____

Building materials _____

Height _____Overall condition _____

Historical total of Head lightkeepers _____
☐ Fog horns/signals   ☐ Working
☐ Visited inside lighthouse ☐ Visited inside lantern room
☐ Walked on the lantern gallery ☐ Took photos
☐ Gift shop ☐ Purchase _____

_____

Favorite facts and lore _____

_____

_____

_____

_____

_____

_____

Special Events _____

_____

Nature, walks or other attractions during the visit

_____

_____

_____

More notes / Sketches / Photos / Postcards

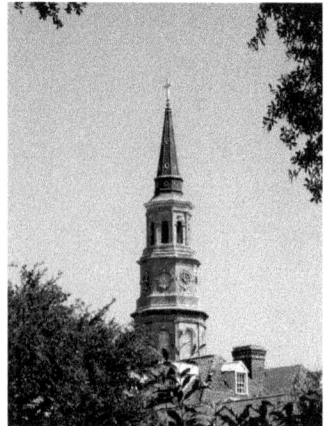

St. Philip's Episcopal Church - Fort Sumter
Range Rear, Charleston, South Carolina

1893. Light inactive since 1915. Church built
in 1838, steeple added in the late 1840s. One
of only two churches in the U.S. to be used as a
lighthouse. The other is the First Baptist Church
of Beverly, Massachusetts. Original light was a
white lantern, later a gas burner in a locomotive
headlight. National Register of Historic Places.
Site open, tower closed.

Weather ___ ☀ ___ ⛅ ___ 🌧 ___ 🌧 ___ 🌨

Lighthouse/Station _____

_____ Visit date _____

Location _____

Maintained by _____

☐ Restored/Date _____ ☐ Original lens still working

Fee/donation: $ _____ ☐ Docent/story teller

☐ Lighthouse ☐ Lightstation ☐ Originally a "family" or a
☐ "stag" lighthouse/station

Date built _____ Date originally lit _____

Illumination type (lens & order)_____

Signal characteristics _____

Focal plane _____Geographic range _____

Lens in operation from _____to _____

☐ Decommissioned/Date _____ ☐ Relit _____

☐ Lens removed from lantern room ☐ Displayed onsite or

☐ offsite _____

☐ Replaced by fixed beacon   ☐ No lens remains

Type of lamp(s) in its history _____

Fuels used in its history _____

Building materials _____

Height _____Overall condition _____

Historical total of Head lightkeepers _____

☐ Fog horns/signals   ☐ Working
☐ Visited inside lighthouse ☐ Visited inside lantern room
☐ Walked on the lantern gallery ☐ Took photos
☐ Gift shop ☐ Purchase _____

_____

Favorite facts and lore _____

_____

_____

_____

_____

_____

_____

Special Events _____

_____

Nature, walks or other attractions during the visit

_____

_____

_____

More notes / Sketches / Photos / Postcards

Halfmoon Reef - Port Lavaca, Texas

1858. Inactive since 1942. Decorative light.
Hexagonal, wooden building and tower.
Round lantern. A screwpile light in Mada-
gorda Bay until damaged in a hurricane
in 1942. Relocated onshore and sold. In
1978, the owner gave the lighthouse to the
Calhoun County Historical Commission.
Relocated again, this time to Port Lavaca
Community Park where is serves as the
local visitor's center. Site and lighthouse
open daily.

Weather ___ ☀ ___ ⛅ ___ 🌧 ___ 🌧 ___ 🌨

Lighthouse/Station _____

_____ Visit date _____

Location _____

Maintained by _____

☐ Restored/Date _____ ☐ Original lens still working

Fee/donation: $ _____ ☐ Docent/story teller

☐ Lighthouse ☐ Lightstation ☐ Originally a "family" or a
☐ "stag" lighthouse/station

Date built _____ Date originally lit _____

Illumination type (lens & order)_____

Signal characteristics _____

Focal plane _____Geographic range _____

Lens in operation from _____to _____

☐ Decommissioned/Date _____ ☐ Relit _____

☐ Lens removed from lantern room ☐ Displayed onsite or

☐ offsite _____

☐ Replaced by fixed beacon ☐ No lens remains

Type of lamp(s) in its history _____

Fuels used in its history _____

Building materials _____

Height _____Overall condition _____

Historical total of Head lightkeepers _____
☐ Fog horns/signals   ☐ Working
☐ Visited inside lighthouse   ☐ Visited inside lantern room
☐ Walked on the lantern gallery   ☐ Took photos
☐ Gift shop ☐ Purchase _____

_____

Favorite facts and lore _____

_____

_____

_____

_____

_____

_____

_____

Special Events _____

_____

Nature, walks or other attractions during the visit

_____

_____

_____

More notes / Sketches / Photos / Postcards

Lighthouse tower shapes: Conical, square, hexagonal, triangular, round, "dumbell" (Lake Pontchartrain), octagonal, skeletal steel or iron frame (square, triangular, square octagonal, octagonal pyramidal).

Burlington Breakwater North
Burlington, Vermont

1857. Active. Lake Champlain. 2003 replica of 1890 lighthouse. Square, pyrmidal structure. Fog horns and beacon. Can be viewed from Burlington's fishing pier. Lighthouse sits on a detached dreakwater near the Burlington ferry terminal. Accessible only by boat. Site open, tower closed. Owner/site manager: City of Burlington.

Weather ___ ☀ ___ ⛅ ___ 🌧 ___ ⛈ ___ 🌨

Lighthouse/Station _____

_____ Visit date _____

Location _____

Maintained by _____

☐ Restored/Date _____ ☐ Original lens still working

Fee/donation: $ _____ ☐ Docent/story teller

☐ Lighthouse ☐ Lightstation ☐ Originally a "family" or a
☐ "stag" lighthouse/station

Date built _____ Date originally lit _____

Illumination type (lens & order) _____

Signal characteristics _____

Focal plane _____ Geographic range _____

Lens in operation from _____ to _____

☐ Decommissioned/Date _____ ☐ Relit _____

☐ Lens removed from lantern room ☐ Displayed onsite or

☐ offsite _____

☐ Replaced by fixed beacon ☐ No lens remains

Type of lamp(s) in its history _____

Fuels used in its history _____

Building materials _____

Height _____ Overall condition _____

Historical total of Head lightkeepers _____
☐ Fog horns/signals ☐ Working
☐ Visited inside lighthouse ☐ Visited inside lantern room
☐ Walked on the lantern gallery ☐ Took photos
☐ Gift shop ☐ Purchase _____

_____

Favorite facts and lore _____

_____

_____

_____

_____

_____

_____

Special Events _____

_____

Nature, walks or other attractions during the visit

_____

_____

_____

More notes / Sketches / Photos / Postcards

Cape Henry Light
Virginia Beach, Virginia

Two lighthouses. 1792: First lighthouse
built by the federal government. Inactive.
Well preserved, octagonal, Federal period
of sandstone. National Historic Landmark,
within Fort Story. Open to public. Passes
and i.d. required.

1881. Active. Built to replace original,
which was cracked. Cast iron over brick. 1st
order Fresnel lens in use. Unusual black and
white stripe "daymarks." First U.S. lighthouse with a radio beacon. No access.

Weather ___ ☀ ___ ☁ ___ 🌧 ___ 🌧 ___ 🌨

Lighthouse/Station _____

_____ Visit date _____

Location _____

Maintained by _____

☐ Restored/Date _____ ☐ Original lens still working

Fee/donation: $ _____ ☐ Docent/story teller

☐ Lighthouse ☐ Lightstation ☐ Originally a "family" or a ☐ "stag" lighthouse/station

Date built _____ Date originally lit _____

Illumination type (lens & order)_____

Signal characteristics _____

Focal plane _____Geographic range _____

Lens in operation from _____to _____

☐ Decommissioned/Date _____ ☐ Relit _____

☐ Lens removed from lantern room ☐ Displayed onsite or

☐ offsite _____

☐ Replaced by fixed beacon ☐ No lens remains

Type of lamp(s) in its history _____

Fuels used in its history _____

Building materials _____

Height _____Overall condition _____

Historical total of Head lightkeepers _____
☐ Fog horns/signals   ☐ Working
☐ Visited inside lighthouse ☐ Visited inside lantern room
☐ Walked on the lantern gallery ☐ Took photos
☐ Gift shop ☐ Purchase _____

_____

Favorite facts and lore _____

_____

_____

_____

_____

_____

_____

Special Events _____

_____

Nature, walks or other attractions during the visit

_____

_____

_____

More notes / Sketches / Photos / Postcards

Grays Harbor Light
Westport, Washington

1898. Active. The state's tallest tower.
Original Henry-Lepaute, 3rd order, clamshell Fresnel lens now fixed in the lantern.
Light currently emits from a FA-251 lens
on the balcony. Fresnel lens lit on special
occasions. The site, museum and tower are
open to public.

Weather ___ ☀ ___ ⛅ ___ ⛈ ___ 🌧 ___ 🌨

Lighthouse/Station _____

_____ Visit date _____

Location _____

Maintained by _____

☐ Restored/Date _____ ☐ Original lens still working

Fee/donation: $ _____ ☐ Docent/story teller

☐ Lighthouse ☐ Lightstation ☐ Originally a "family" or a
☐ "stag" lighthouse/station

Date built _____ Date originally lit _____

Illumination type (lens & order)_____

Signal characteristics _____

Focal plane _____Geographic range _____

Lens in operation from _____to _____

☐ Decommissioned/Date _____ ☐ Relit _____

☐ Lens removed from lantern room ☐ Displayed onsite or

☐ offsite _____

☐ Replaced by fixed beacon ☐ No lens remains

Type of lamp(s) in its history _____

Fuels used in its history _____

Building materials _____

Height _____Overall condition _____

Historical total of Head lightkeepers _____
- ☐ Fog horns/signals   ☐ Working
- ☐ Visited inside lighthouse ☐ Visited inside lantern room
- ☐ Walked on the lantern gallery ☐ Took photos
- ☐ Gift shop ☐ Purchase _____

_____

Favorite facts and lore _____

_____

_____

_____

_____

_____

_____

Special Events _____

_____

Nature, walks or other attractions during the visit

_____

_____

_____

More notes / Sketches / Photos / Postcards

National Lighthouse Day: Annually on August 7th. "This day in 1789, the Ninth Act of the First Congress established federal control of lighthouses. Passed and signed by President George Washington."
U.S. Lighthouse Society

Cana Island Lighthouse
Door County, Wisconsin

1870. Active. Original 3rd order, Henry Lepaute, Fresnel lens still in use. Keeper's house museum. Other outbuildings remain. 300-foot natural causeway leads to the lighthouse, but can be flooded at times. Lard oil was replaced by mineral oil in 1882, later by kerosene. Site open, keeper's house museum, oil house, and tower open daily in season. Manager: Door County Maritime Museum.

Weather ___ ☀ ___ ⛅ ___ 🌧 ___ 🌧 ___ 🌨

Lighthouse/Station _____

_____ Visit date _____

Location _____

Maintained by _____

☐ Restored/Date _____ ☐ Original lens still working

Fee/donation: $ _____ ☐ Docent/story teller

☐ Lighthouse ☐ Lightstation ☐ Originally a "family" or a
☐ "stag" lighthouse/station

Date built _____ Date originally lit _____

Illumination type (lens & order)_____

Signal characteristics _____

Focal plane _____Geographic range _____

Lens in operation from _____to _____

☐ Decommissioned/Date _____ ☐ Relit _____

☐ Lens removed from lantern room ☐ Displayed onsite or

☐ offsite _____

☐ Replaced by fixed beacon ☐ No lens remains

Type of lamp(s) in its history _____

Fuels used in its history _____

Building materials _____

Height _____Overall condition _____

Historical total of Head lightkeepers _____
☐ Fog horns/signals   ☐ Working
☐ Visited inside lighthouse ☐ Visited inside lantern room
☐ Walked on the lantern gallery ☐ Took photos
☐ Gift shop ☐ Purchase _____

_____

Favorite facts and lore _____

_____

_____

_____

_____

_____

_____

Special Events _____

_____

Nature, walks or other attractions during the visit

_____

_____

_____

More notes / Sketches / Photos / Postcards

Castillo San Felipe del Morro Lighthouse
San Juan, Puerto Rico

1846. Active. Oldest lighthouse in Puerto Rico.
Light was built on the original fort, Castillo San
Juan Felipe del Morro, begun over 400 years ago.
In 1876, the light was moved to Ochoa Bastion and
rebuilt as a cast iron structure. In March 1899 the
U.S. Navy rebuilt the tower in concrete. Replaced in
1908 with the present tower. 3rd order Fresnel lens
(1899) in use. Restored 1991. Site open, light closed.
Managed by the National Park Service.

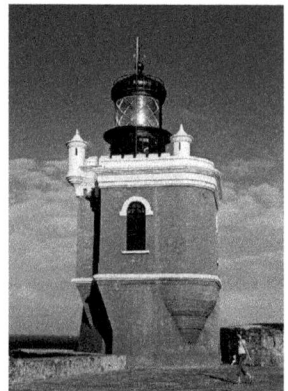

Weather ___ ☀ ___ ⛅ ___ 🌧 ___ ⛈ ___ 🌨

Lighthouse/Station _____

_____ Visit date _____

Location _____

Maintained by _____

☐ Restored/Date _____ ☐ Original lens still working

Fee/donation: $ _____ ☐ Docent/story teller

☐ Lighthouse ☐ Lightstation ☐ Originally a "family" or a
☐ "stag" lighthouse/station

Date built _____ Date originally lit _____

Illumination type (lens & order)_____

Signal characteristics _____

Focal plane _____Geographic range _____

Lens in operation from _____to _____

☐ Decommissioned/Date _____ ☐ Relit _____

☐ Lens removed from lantern room ☐ Displayed onsite or

☐ offsite _____

☐ Replaced by fixed beacon ☐ No lens remains

Type of lamp(s) in its history _____

Fuels used in its history _____

Building materials _____

Height _____Overall condition _____

Historical total of Head lightkeepers _____

☐ Fog horns/signals ☐ Working

☐ Visited inside lighthouse ☐ Visited inside lantern room

☐ Walked on the lantern gallery ☐ Took photos

☐ Gift shop ☐ Purchase _____

_____

Favorite facts and lore _____

_____

_____

_____

_____

_____

_____

Special Events _____

_____

Nature, walks or other attractions during the visit

_____

_____

_____

More notes / Sketches / Photos / Postcards

Want to Know More About Lighthouses?

Check online for individual lighthouse, support organizations, and programs.

University of North Carolina's "Lighthouse Directory": information on more than 18,600 lighthouses around the world. Individual lighthouse writeups contain links to other websites for more facts, history, and images. Monthly lighthouse news. A star system (0 to 4 stars) rates each lighthouse based on accessibility and facilities. Clear definition: "What is a lighthouse?"

https://www.unc.edu/~rowlett/lighthouse/

Lighthouse Friends: U.S. and Canadian lighthouses. 15 search filters and icons for information such as accessibility, museum or open interiors, active lens, fees, hauntings, stays available. Matching icons on each lighthouse page. Lights by state, maps by light, maps of lights that offer lodging or lightkeeper opportunities. Lighthouse Friends app through Googleplay.

www.lighthousefriends.com

U.S. Lighthouse Society: Memberships assist the Society in its educational and restoration support work. The group conducts research and offers financial (grants program) and non-financial help to organizations restoring lighthouses across the nation. Collect stamped impressions at each lighthouse you visit as part of the Society's "Lighthouse Passport Program" (see website for a list). Site has a "Kid's Corner," and a Glossary of terms in its Facts and Trivia section and much more. Membership includes the quarterly, "The Keeper's Log Journal."

www.uslhs.org

Lighthouse Preservation Society: Membership. Northeast lighthouse focus, while working to make lighthouse preservation and restoration a national issue. The Society's misson is to preserve historic lighthouse structures for future generations, to open them to public use and enjoyment, and to document their history and that of their keepers." Lobbied and won Congressional support for National Lighthouse Day. Nominated 25 lighthouses for U.S. postage stamps.

http://www.lighthousepreservation.org/index.php

Lighthouse Digest: bi-monthly magazine: http://lighthousedigest.com

U.S. Coast Guard: A valuable lighthouse partner. Historic and current information on lighthouses, the Light House Service, historic photography, a list of Fresnel lenses still in operation (as of 2008), and much more.

http://www.uscg.mil/history/h_lhindex.asp

A Very Short Book List

Lighthouse-related books abound—non-fiction and fiction—for all ages. Search for websites and videos devoted to lighthouse and Fresnel lens history, restorations, and operations.

Lighthouses of the World by Lisa Purcell, Skyhorse Publishing

A Short Bright Flash: Augustin Fresnel and the Birth of the Modern Lighthouse by Theresa Levitt, W. W. Norton & Company

Ghostly Beacons: Haunted Lighthouses of North America by Therese Lanigan-Schmidt, Schiffer Publishing, Ltd

Your local bookstore, library or online book sites have multiple lighthouse-related titles by the following authors:

Lost Lighthouses: Stories and Images of America's Vanished Lighthouses by Tim Harrison and Ray Jones

The Lighthouse Encyclopedia: The Definitive Reference by Ray Jones Globe Pequot Press

The Lighthouse Almanac by Elinor DeWire, Sentinel Publications

Women Who Kept the Lights: An Illustrated History of Female Lighthouse Keepers by Mary Louise Clifford and J. Candace Clifford, Cypress Communications

Haunted Lighthouses: Phantom Keepers, Ghostly Shipwrecks, and Sinister Calls From The Deep by Ray Jones, Globe Pequot Press

CHILDREN'S BOOKS: many non-fiction, fiction, and coloring books. One K-4 teaching resource (based on Lighthouse Society's booklets) is available at the US Coast Guard site. http://www.uscg.mil/history/articles/lighthousecurriculum.pdf

Maps

Physical maps:

United States Lighthouses: Every Standing Lighthouse in All 50 States
Bella Terra Publishing, LLC P.O. Box 731 Rhinebeck, NY 12572

http://bellaterraMaps.com/lighthouses.html

Bella Terra also offers: *Northwest Lighhouses - Oregon, Washington, and Alaska; California/Hawaii Lightouses; Florida; Maine; Massachusetts & Rhode Island; Mid-Atlantic; Southeast*

Online maps:

Lighhouse Friends - U.S. and Canada - http://lighhousefriends.com

Connecticut:
   http://lighthousemaps.com/

U.S. Lighhouse Society -
   http://uslhs.org/lighthouse-interactive-resources

Historic Nautical Charts -
   http://www.nauticalchartsonline.com/charts/historical/All

NOAA charts -
   http://historicalcharts.noaa.gov/

Apps:

U.S. Lights by Kraig Anderson. (Lighthousefriends.com) Maps, historic and current information. Sort by state. Also Canadian Lighthouses app. Available through Googleplay.

Lighthouse Locator by MapMuse: Maps and searches. Track your visits and photos. Available through iTunes.

*Collecting Lighthouse postage stamps, covers, cancels, and cachets —
US and Foreign:* Lighthouse Stamp Society and other sellers. Collect a few
and add or list on the provided pages. http://lighthousestampsociety.org/wp/

Join the U.S. Lighthouse Society's Passport Program, adding stamped pages to
your passport at each participating lighthouse you visit. Buy passport books at
lighthouses or through USLHS's website. http://uslhs.org/fun/passport-club

Photography: Lighthouses offer wonderful opportunities for photographers.
Their forms, settings, and lights are all different. Plan ahead with a theme in
mind and take shots of one subject from several angles. Architecture,
mechanics, decoration, interior designs are all features that tell a visual story
as backdrop to the human and cultural lives of each light or station. Are there
zoom shots that isolate and explore details the viewer doesn't otherwise see?
What about the environment surrounding the lighthouse or station? Can you
capture what made this spot perilous, isolated, or comfortable for sailors and
keepers? Record your themes and make a digital or print album.

Writing: Poetry or prose, songs. See if you can write beyond the general
information you collect on your visits. Was there something about the
weather that moved you, maybe cloud formations? Perhaps an historic event
about a lightkeeper, the light, or a rescue sparks your imagination. Free-write
the first draft, don't worry that it's not good, certainly not perfect, just get
something down close to the moment. You can build on and correct it later.
Use these pages or a separate notebook or a digital
device to capture your thoughts.

Artwork: Draw, paint, collage what you see, feel
or both. The pages here are suitable for pencil, pen,
colored pencils, and crayon, but not wet media.
Use any blank page to make premiminary sketches
for a project to finish later.

Help save our lights: Share your experiences and
creative work with others. Donate, volunteer or
vacation at a lighthouse. The more people visit our
remaining lighthouses, the better chance these
beacons on the past will enjoy a future.

Creative space, notes, photo themes, doodles...

Creative space, notes, photo themes, doodles...

Lighthouse Stays

Date, Where, Type (guest lodger or volunteer "keeper"), Memories

_____

_____

_____

_____

_____

_____

_____

_____

_____

_____

_____

_____

_____

_____

_____

_____

Lighthouse Stays

Date, Where, Type (guest lodger or volunteer "keeper"), Memories

_____

_____

_____

_____

_____

_____

_____

_____

_____

_____

_____

_____

_____

_____

_____

Lighthouse Stays

Date, Where, Type (guest lodger or volunteer "keeper"), Memories

_____

_____

_____

_____

_____

_____

_____

_____

_____

_____

_____

_____

_____

_____

_____

_____

_____

Lighthouse Stays

Date, Where, Type (guest lodger or volunteer "keeper"), Memories

_____

_____

_____

_____

_____

_____

_____

_____

_____

_____

_____

_____

_____

_____

_____

_____

_____

_____

Lighthouse Stays

Date, Where, Type (guest lodger or volunteer "keeper"), Memories

_____

_____

_____

_____

_____

_____

_____

_____

_____

_____

_____

_____

_____

_____

_____

_____

_____

_____

Lighthouse Stays

Date, Where, Type (guest lodger or volunteer "keeper"), Memories

_____

_____

_____

_____

_____

_____

_____

_____

_____

_____

_____

_____

_____

_____

_____

_____

_____

Lighthouse Stays

Date, Where, Type (guest lodger or volunteer "keeper"), Memories

Lighthouse Stays

Date, Where, Type (guest lodger or volunteer "keeper"), Memories

My Lighthouse Stamps - Domestic & Foreign

Paste in or keep a list

My Lighthouse Stamps - Domestic & Foreign

Paste in or keep a list

My Lighthouse Miniatures & Other Collectables
log what, when, and where you got your treasures

_____

_____

_____

_____

_____

_____

_____

_____

_____

_____

_____

_____

_____

_____

_____

My Lighthouse Miniatures & Other Collectables
log what, when, and where you got your treasures

_____

_____

_____

_____

_____

_____

_____

_____

_____

_____

_____

_____

_____

_____

_____

_____

_____

My Lighthouse Miniatures & Other Collectables
log what, when, and where you got your treasures

_____

_____

_____

_____

_____

_____

_____

_____

_____

_____

_____

_____

_____

_____

Creative space, notes, photo themes, doodles...

Glossary

A short list of terms used in and around lighthouses. For a complete glossary, visit the U.S. Lighthouse Society link below.

Aerobeacon: A long-distance, stationary or rotating searchlight. Cheaper to produce than Fresnel lens and adopted by many lighthouses.

Aid to Navigation: Any external device, assisting a navigator in determining location or to warn of dangers. Federal aids are owned and maintained by the U.S. Coast Guard. Private aids rest in private hands, decommissioned, and sometimes relit as historical sites.

Arc of Visibility: The part of the horizon over which a lighted aid to navigation is visible from seaward.

Automated: A lighthouse operated without a keeper. Light controlled by light or fog conditions or via timers.

Characteristic: Color, sound, or electronic signals identifying individual lighthouses, buoys, or other aids to navigation.

Clockwork Mechanism: Historic clocklike mechanisms of gears, pulleys, and weights reset by the lightkeepers at timed intervals to keep the lens turning.

Decommissioned: A lighthouse which no longer functions as an official aid to navigation.

Establish: To authorize, for the first time, a particular official aid to navigation.

Focal Plane: Horizontal beam sent through the focus of an illuminating lens. Distance from the focal plane to the water is the "height of the focal plane."

Fog Signal: Manual or electronic warning device used in periods of dense fog when the light flash would not be visible to mariners.

Fresnel Lens: Stepped section lens made of convex lenses and prisims. Invented by Augustin Fresnel.

Gallery: The walkway around the outside of the lantern room or watch room.

Geographic Range: The greatest distance an aid to navigation can be seen, given the earth's curvature, height of aid and the viewer.

Keeper: The person who maintains the light and often the lighthouse and surrounding grounds and buildings.

Lantern: The glass enclosure surrounding the light.

Lens: Optical system used to concentrate light. The "order" is the lens size, which determines the brightness of the beam and extent of its reach.

For full lists visit: http://uslhs.org/education/glossaries-facts-trivia

Glossary

Lamp: The part inside the lens that creates the light.

Lighthouse: Tower built with an enclosed light used as an aid to navigation.

Light Station: A collection of buildings, including the lighthouse, keeper's houses, and support structures.

Parapet: A railed walkway surrounding the lantern room.

Revolving Light: A turning light that produces a characteristic flash.

Stag Light: A lighthouse maintained by one, unmarried keeper.

Ventilator: The round ball-shaped exhaust and ventillation cap on top of the lantern room roof of many lighthouses.

Watch Room: Often directly below the lantern room, this space allowed the keeper to watch the weather and storm conditions.

Wickie: A nickname given to keepers when lenses were illuminated by fuel-operated wicks.

Add your own terms

_____

_____

_____

_____

_____

_____

_____

_____

_____

Glossary

Creative space, notes, photo themes, doodles…

Former Executive Director of the Yolo County, California Resource Conservation District, Katy Pye now lives and writes on California's North Coast. Intrigued by her family's and local 19th century maritime histories, she volunteers at the Point Cabrillo Light Station State Historic Park. Camera in hand, spring is her favorite time, searching for rare and common plants in the sometimes harsh, but always beautiful bluff landscape near the Light Station. The brilliant Fresnel flash is a welcome beacon on many of her daily walks.

• • • • •

Katy is also the author of *Elizabeth's Landing*, winner of four, international book awards. Her website, blog, and books support sea turtles and young people dedicated to a better world.

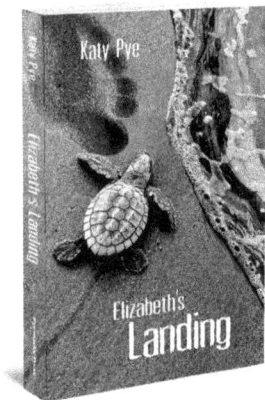

Adrift, 14 year-old Elizabeth sparks Texas-sized trouble, fighting power and history to save sea turtles, family, and find her way home.

Elizabeth's Landing is available in print and e-book formats. Four chapters and a discussion guide are free at:
   katypye.com/elizabeths-landing
She can be reached through the website's *Contact Me* page.

Looking down the St. Augustine Lighthouse staircase

S.W. Clyde image - public domain